MASTER THE ART OF FACEBOOK MARKETING

AND GROW YOUR STARTUP BUSINESS LIKE CRAZY

CHIRAG MARLECHA

Made with ♥ on the Notion Press Platform
www.notionpress.com

" To all the Entrepreneurs and Small Business Owners, who have the courage to take a chance on their Dreams and turn them into Reality.

May this Book serve as a Guide and Inspiration to help you Grow your Business with the Power of Facebook Marketing.

To my Mentors, for always Believing in me and for being a Constant Source of Guidance and Support in my Journey.

Your Teachings will stay with me forever.

And finally, to my Family, who has always been there for me, Cheering me on, and Supporting me in all my endeavors.

This Book is Dedicated to you, with Love and Gratitude. "

Contents

Contents

Gratitude & Thanks Giving

I am Greatful, Thankful & Blessed

To have a such a Founderful Parents

Who gave me the Freedom to Choose my Career

Leela Pincha my GrandMother (My Inspiration)

Arun Marlecha my Dad (My Hero)

Anjana Arun my Mom (My Best Mentor in my Life)

and
Of Course yes My Younger Brother

Viraat – He is my Younger Brother, My Business Partner, My Bestie &

Sometimes a Coach for me...

Preface

As many of you know, I have a passion for entrepreneurship and for helping businesses grow. In this book, I share my experiences and insights on how you can use Facebook to grow your startup. Whether you're just starting out, or you've been in business for a while, this book is packed with practical tips, tricks, and strategies that you can use to grow your business.

I wrote this book with the intention of making it easy for anyone to understand, even if you have no prior experience with Facebook marketing. The strategies in this book are designed to be actionable, so you can start seeing results right away.

My Mentors

1. Gopal Krishnan

2. Siddharth Rajsekar

3. Purushottam Hambarde

4. Himanshu Agarwal

5. Grant Cardone

6. Dan Lok

7. Millionaire Magesh

8. Zubin

9. Sorav Jain

About The Author

Hi i am Chirag Marlecha

I am an Author, Speaker, Digital Marketer, Video Editor,
Animator, Multimedia Specialist, Graphic Designer
and I am Just 17yrs (in the year 2022)

I Have Mentored Startups, Small Scale Businesses, Coaches,
Teachers, College Students & Homemakers about Facebook
Marketing

I am Passionate About

Cars, Bikes, Luxury Products, Travelling, Exploring, Swimming,
New Technology

& A Big Foodie

Who Is This Book For?

This Book is Specially Designed for anyone
who wants to Sell Products or Services.
No matter which Industry you are in...

It Works Perfectly For...

1. Small business owners
2. E-Commerce store owners
3. B2b or b2c lead generation
4. Coaches and trainers
5. Agency owners
6. Consultants
7. Doctors / dentists
8. Entrepreneurs
9. Real estate
10. Makeup artist
11. Digital marketers
12. Starting a business
13. Local businesses
14. Affiliate marketers
15. Freelancers
16. Information products
17. Social media marketers
18. Self employed
19. Homemakers
20. And anyone who wants to generate leads or sales

Chapter – 1
INTRODUCTION

Let's Begin

A – Why Facebook marketing is a Valuable Tool for Startups

A - Why Facebook marketing is a Valuable Tool for Startups

Facebook is the largest social media platform in the world,

with over 2.9 billion monthly active users.

This means that it offers a huge potential audience for businesses of all sizes, including startups.

In addition to its large user base,

Facebook also has a number of features and tools that make it particularly useful for startups looking to grow and reach new customers.

One of the main benefits of using Facebook for marketing is the Ability to Target Specific Groups of Users.

With Facebook's advanced targeting options, businesses can reach users based on Demographics, Interests, Behaviors, and More.

This allows startups to focus their marketing efforts on the most relevant and likely to convert audience, increasing the chances of success.

Facebook is also a highly visual platform, making it ideal for businesses that have visually appealing products or services to promote.

The platform allows Businesses to share Photos, Videos, and Other Types of Rich Media to showcase their Offerings in a way that is Engaging & Interactive.

Finally, Facebook offers a variety of Tools and Features specifically designed to help Businesses Reach and Engage with Customers, including Advertising Options, Messenger, and Instagram.

By leveraging these tools and features, startups can create a comprehensive and effective Facebook marketing strategy that helps them grow and succeed.

B - Setting clear Goals for your Facebook Marketing efforts

SETTING CLEAR GOALS FOR YOUR FACEBOOK MARKETING EFFORTS

B - Setting clear Goals for your Facebook Marketing efforts

Before Starting any Marketing Campaign,

It's important to have a clear understanding of what you hope to achieve.

This is especially true for Startups, which often have limited resources and

need to make the most of every marketing dollar.

By setting clear goals for your Facebook marketing efforts, you can ensure that your efforts are

focused and aligned with your overall business objectives.

Some examples of Goals that you might set for your Facebook marketing efforts include:

Increasing brand awareness:

Using Facebook to reach new users and get your brand in front of more people.

Generating leads:

Using Facebook to collect contact information from potential customers and add them to your email list.

Driving traffic to your website:

Using Facebook to promote your website and encourage users to visit it.

Boosting sales:

Using Facebook to drive direct sales or promote special offers.

By setting specific, measurable, achievable, relevant, and time-bound (SMART) goals,

you can ensure that your Facebook marketing efforts are focused and have a clear sense of direction.

This will help you track your progress and make adjustments as needed to ensure that you are meeting your goals.

Chapter – 2 Creating a Facebook Business Page

Let's Begin

A - Setting up a Business Page On Facebook

Setting up a Business Page on Facebook

A - Setting up a Business Page On Facebook

Go to **facebook.com/business** and

Click on "**Create**"

Select "**Page**" from the dropdown menu and

Choose the **Category that Best Represents your Business.**

Enter your **Business Name** and

Select a **Page Username**

(**Which will appear as a URL for your page**).

Add a **Profile Picture** and **Cover Photo**

That Represents your Business.

Fill out the "**About**" section with a Brief Description of your
Business and any Relevant Information

Such as your **Website** or **Contact Information.**

INVITE YOUR FRIENDS AND FOLLOWERS TO LIKE YOUR PAGE.

Once you've set up your Business Page,

It's Important to keep it up to date with

Fresh Content and **Information about your Business.**

You can do this by

Posting Updates, Photos, and Other Content related to your Business, as well as responding to Comments and Messages from Users.

By regularly updating and engaging with your followers, you can build a loyal community of followers who are interested in your business and what you have to offer.

B - Optimizing your Business Page For maximum Visibility & Engagement

OPTIMIZING YOUR PAGE FOR MAXIMUM VISIBILITY AND ENGAGEMENT

B - Optimizing your Business Page For maximum Visibility & Engagement

Complete your Page's Information:

Make sure to fill out all relevant fields in the "About" section of your page, including your Business's Address, Phone Number, and Website.

This will help users find and contact your business more easily.

Use keywords in your Page's Name and About Section:

Include relevant keywords in your Page's Name and About Section to make it easier for users to find your business when searching on Facebook.

Use a clear profile picture and cover photo:

Choose a Profile Picture and Cover Photo that accurately represents your Business and is visually appealing.

This will help your page stand out and make a good impression on users.

Post regularly:

To keep your followers engaged and interested in your business, try to post regular updates and content related to your industry.

Use hashtags:

Including relevant hashtags in your posts can make it easier for users to discover your content and can also help increase the visibility of your posts.

Engage with your followers:

Respond to comments and messages from users, & make an effort to like & comment on their posts as well.

This can help build a sense of community and encourage more users to follow and engage with your page.

By following these optimization tips, you can increase the visibility and engagement of your business page and effectively reach more users on Facebook.

Chapter – 3 Developing a Facebook Content Strategy

Let's Begin

A – Identifying your Target Audience On Facebook

Identifying Your Target Audience on Facebook

A - Identifying your Target Audience On Facebook

Identifying your Target Audience is an important first step in developing a content strategy on Facebook.

Your Target Audience is the group of users that you most want to reach and engage with your business.

By understanding who your target audience is, you can create content that resonates with them and meets their needs and interests.

There are several ways to identify your target audience on Facebook:

Define your customer avatar:

Create a detailed profile of your ideal customer, including their demographics, interests, behaviors, and pain points.

This can help you understand what type of content and messaging is most likely to appeal to them.

Use Facebook's Audience Insights tool:

This tool allows you to analyze the demographics, interests, and behaviors of users on Facebook.

You can use this data to identify common characteristics among your current followers and tailor your content to attract similar users.

Monitor your page's insights:

Facebook provides data on the demographics and interests of your page's followers in the page insights section.

You can use this data to understand who is most engaged with your page and tailor your content accordingly.

By identifying your target audience on Facebook, you can create content that speaks directly to their needs and interests, increasing the chances of engagement and success.

B – Crafting a Content Calendar that Resonates with your Audience

Crafting a Content Calendar that Resonates with Your Audience

B - Crafting a Content Calendar that Resonates with your Audience

A content calendar is a schedule of the content that you plan to post on your Facebook page.

By creating a content calendar, you can ensure that you are consistently posting relevant and

Engaging content that resonates with your target audience.

Here are some tips for crafting a content calendar that Resonates with your audience:

Identify your goals:

Before creating your content calendar, identify your goals for your Facebook marketing efforts.

This will help you focus your content and ensure that it aligns with your overall business objectives.

Know your audience:

Understand the demographics, interests, and needs of your target audience and create content that speaks to them.

Mix up your content:

Don't post the same type of content all the time.

Instead, mix things up by posting a variety of content types, such as text updates, photos, videos, and links.

Plan ahead:

To save time and ensure that you always have content ready to go, try to plan out your content calendar in advance.

This can also help you identify any gaps in your content and come up with ideas to fill them.

By following these tips, you can create a content calendar that resonates with your audience and helps you achieve your marketing goals on Facebook.

C – Planning and Scheduling Posts Using Facebook's Native Tools

Planning and Scheduling Posts Using Facebook's Native Tools

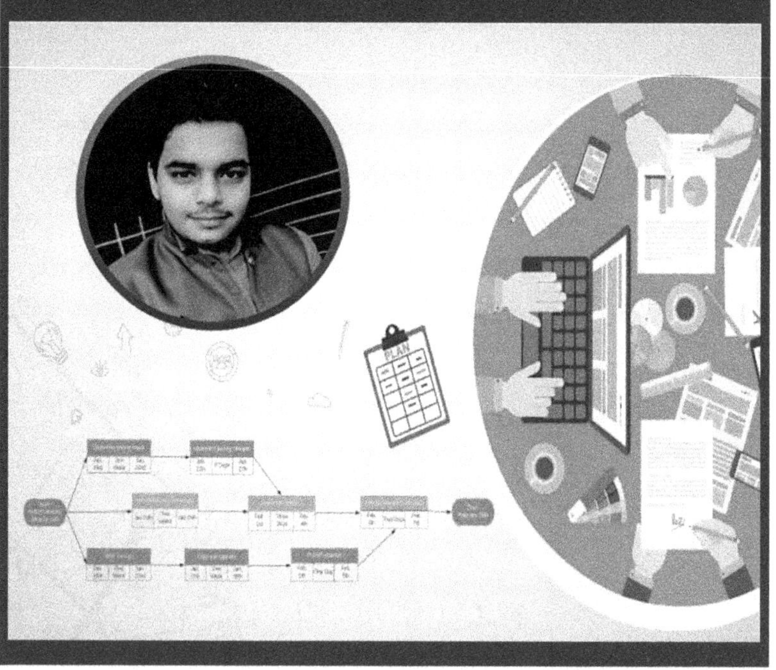

C - Planning and Scheduling Posts Using Facebook's Native Tools

Facebook offers a number of tools and features that can help you plan and schedule your posts in advance.

This can save you time and ensure that you are consistently posting high-quality content on your page.

Here are some tips for planning and scheduling posts using Facebook's native tools:

Use the Facebook Page Scheduler:

This feature allows you to schedule posts to be published at a later date and time.

To schedule a post, simply create the post as you normally would and then click the clock icon in the bottom left corner of the post window.

From there, you can select the date and time that you want the post to be published.

Use the Facebook Creator Studio:

This tool allows you to schedule and publish posts across multiple Facebook pages and Instagram accounts.

It also provides analytics and insights on the performance of your posts.

Use a third-party scheduling tool:

There are a number of third-party tools, such as

Hoot suite and Buffer that allow you to schedule and publish posts on Facebook and other social media platforms.

These tools often offer additional features and functionality, such as the ability to schedule posts in advance and collaborate with team members.

By using these tools to plan and schedule your posts, you can save time and ensure that you are consistently posting high-quality content on your page.

Chapter – 4 Advertising on Facebook

Let's Begin

A – Understanding the Different Types Of Facebook Ads

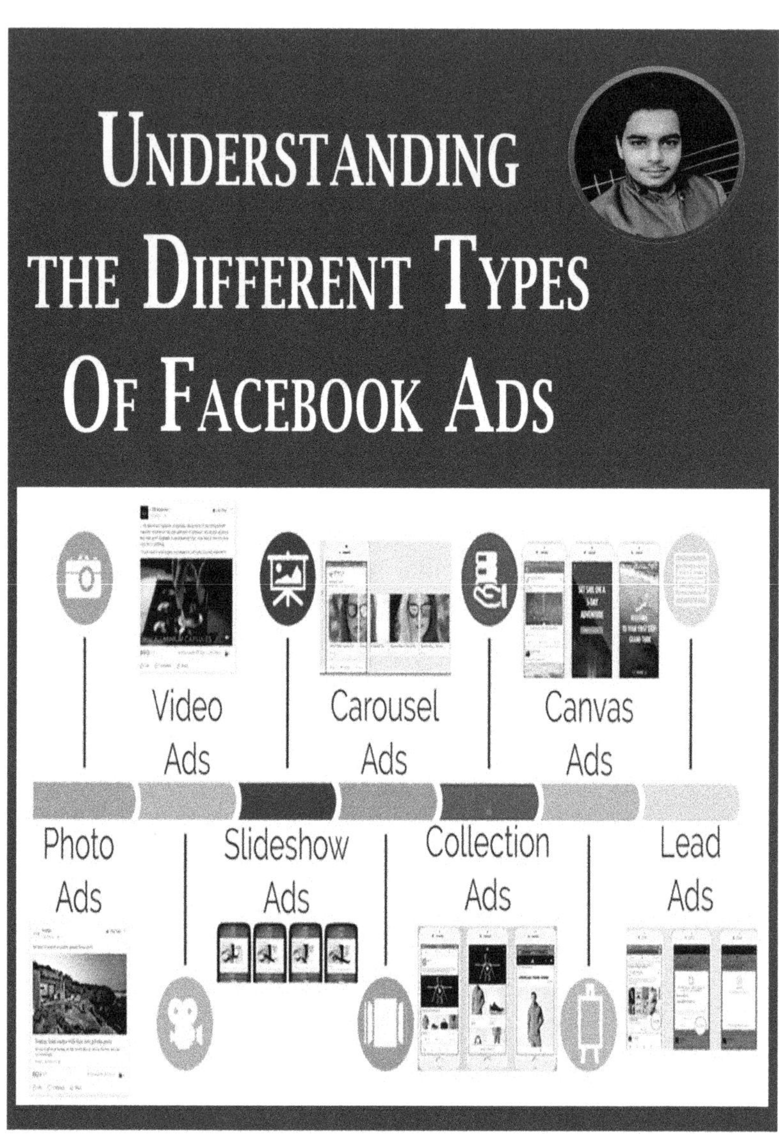

A - Understanding the Different Types Of Facebook Ads

Facebook offers a range of Ad Formats

that Businesses can use to Reach and engage

their Target Audience.

Facebook Advertising is now one of the most effective tools out there to grow your Business, Create Loyal Customers, and Generate Leads and Sales.

There are now over

3 Million Businesses Advertising on Facebook

" And there's never been a better time to start than now. "

Some of the most common types of Facebook ads include:

Image ads:

These are Traditional Ads that consist of a Single Image and Some Accompanying Text.

Image Ads can be used to Promote Products, Services, or Events and can be targeted to Specific Audiences based on Demographics, Interests, and Behaviors.

Video ads:

These are Ads that consist of a Video and some Accompanying Text.

Video ads can be a powerful way to showcase your products or services and can be particularly effective

For telling a story or creating an emotional connection with users.

Carousel ads:

These are ads that consist of a series of images or videos that users can swipe through.

Carousel ads can be used to showcase multiple products or tell a story and can be a particularly effective format for e-commerce businesses.

Slideshow ads:

These are ads that consist of a series of images that are automatically played in a loop, similar to a short video.

Slideshow ads can be a cost-effective way to

create video-like content and can be particularly useful for

businesses with limited video resources.

Collection ads:

These are ads that allow users to browse & purchase products directly from Facebook or Instagram. Collection ads are particularly useful for e-commerce businesses and can help drive direct sales from social media.

By understanding the different ad formats available on Facebook, businesses can choose the best format for their goals and target audience.

B - Setting up a Facebook Ads Account

B - Setting up a Facebook Ads Account

To get started with advertising on Facebook, you'll need to set up a Facebook Ads account.

Here's how:

Go to https://www.facebook.com/business and click on "**Create.**"

Select "**Ads Manager**" from the dropdown menu.

If you don't already have a Facebook Ads account, you'll be prompted to create one.

Click "**Create Account**" and follow the prompts to set up your account.

Once you've set up your Facebook Ads account, you'll be able to create and manage your ad campaigns.

You'll need to specify a Budget for your Campaigns and Choose the Specific Goals and Target Audience for your Ads.

You'll also need to create the actual ad content,

Which can be an Image, Video, or Other Type of Media.

It's a good idea to familiarize yourself with the Facebook Ads platform and its various features before diving into creating campaigns.

C – Creating & Targeting Effective Facebook Ad Campaigns

CREATING & TARGETING EFFECTIVE FACEBOOK AD CAMPAIGNS

C - Creating & Targeting Effective Facebook Ad Campaigns

Once you've set up a Facebook Ads account and determined your advertising goals and target audience,

You can start creating and targeting ad campaigns.

Here are some tips for creating and targeting effective ad campaigns on Facebook:

Use clear and compelling ad copy:

The text in your ad should clearly convey the value of your product or service and convince users to take action.

Use high-quality images or video:

The visuals in your ad should be eye-catching and relevant to your product or service.

Test different ad creatives:

It's a good idea to test multiple versions of your ad (with different images, text, and targeting) to see which performs best.

Use detailed targeting:

Facebook's advanced targeting options allow you to reach specific groups of users based on demographics, interests, behaviors, and more.

Use these options to target your ads to the most relevant and likely to convert audience.

Use retargeting:

Retargeting allows you to show ads to users who have visited your website or interacted with your business in some way.

This can be a powerful way to bring users back to your site and convert them into customers.

By following these tips, you can create and target effective ad campaigns on Facebook that help you achieve your business goals.

Chapter – 5 Measuring & Analysing Your Facebook Marketing Efforts

Let's Begin

A – Using Facebook's built-in analytics Tools to track the Performance of your Posts & Ads

Using Facebook's built-in analytics Tools to track the Performance of your Posts & Ads

A - Using Facebook's built-in analytics Tools to track the Performance of your Posts & Ads

Facebook provides a number of analytics tools

that allow you to track the performance

of your page, posts, and ads.

These tools can help you understand how your content is performing and identify areas for improvement.

To access these tools,

Click on the "**Insights**" tab on your Facebook business page.

From there, you can view a range of metrics,

Including:

Page likes:

The number of users who have liked your page.

Reach:

The number of users who have seen your content.

Engagement:

The number of likes, comments, and shares your content has received.

Traffic:

The number of clicks on links in your posts that have directed users to your website.

You can also use Facebook's Ads Manager to track the performance of your ad campaigns.

This tool provides detailed metrics on the reach, engagement, and conversions generated by your ads.

By regularly tracking and analyzing these metrics, you can understand how your content and ad campaigns are performing and make adjustments as needed to improve their effectiveness.

B – Understanding key metrics like Reach, Engagement, & Conversions

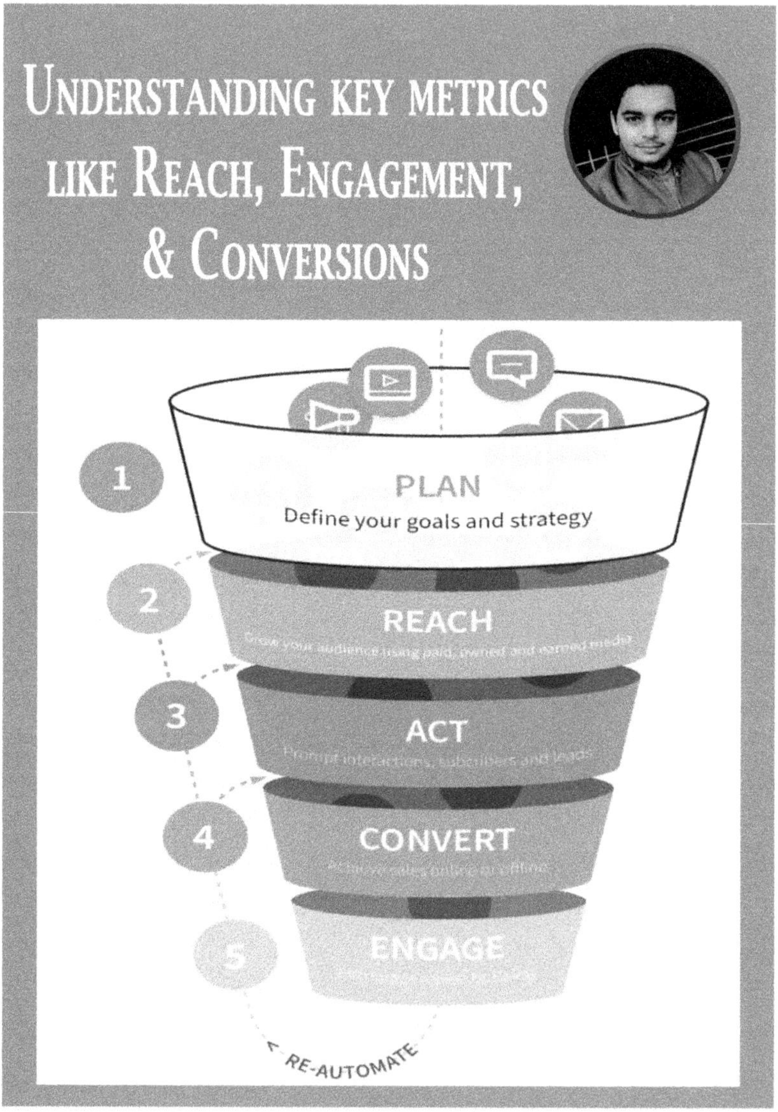

UNDERSTANDING KEY METRICS
LIKE REACH, ENGAGEMENT,
& CONVERSIONS

1
PLAN
Define your goals and strategy
2
REACH
Grow your audience using paid, owned and earned media
3
ACT
Prompt interactions, subscribers and leads
4
CONVERT
Achieve sales online or offline
5
ENGAGE
RE-AUTOMATE

B - Understanding key metrics like Reach, Engagement, & Conversions

Reach:

Reach refers to the number of users who have seen your content.

It's important to track reach to understand the size of your audience on Facebook and the potential impact of your content.

Engagement:

Engagement refers to the number of likes, comments, and shares your content has received.

High engagement is a good sign that your content is resonating with your audience and can help to increase the visibility of your content.

Conversions:

Conversions refer to any desired action that a user takes, such as making a purchase or signing up for an email list.

Tracking conversions can help you understand the effectiveness of your Facebook marketing efforts in driving business outcomes.

Cost per conversion:

This metric measures the cost of your Facebook marketing efforts in relation to the number of conversions generated.

By understanding the cost per conversion, you can determine the return on investment (ROI) of your Facebook marketing efforts and make adjustments as needed to improve efficiency.

By tracking these and other key metrics, you can gain a better understanding of the performance of your Facebook marketing efforts and make informed decisions to improve their effectiveness.

C – Using this Data to continually Improve your Facebook Marketing Strategy

Using this Data to Continually Improve your Facebook Marketing Strategy

C - Using this Data to continually Improve your Facebook Marketing Strategy

Use Google Analytics:

In addition to Facebook's built-in analytics tools, you can also use Google Analytics to track the performance of your Facebook marketing efforts.

Google Analytics can provide detailed data on the traffic and conversions generated from Facebook, as well as the behavior of users who visit your site from the platform.

Use UTM parameters:

UTM (Urchin Tracking Module) parameters are tags that you can add to the links in your Facebook posts to track the performance of specific campaigns or content.

By using UTM parameters, you can see how much traffic and conversions specific Facebook posts are generating and make more informed decisions about your content strategy.

A/B test your content:

A/B testing involves creating two versions of a piece of content (such as two different Facebook posts) and comparing their performance.

This can help you understand which types of content are most effective at driving engagement and conversions.

Monitor your page's insights:

Facebook's page insights feature provides data on the demographics and interests of your page's followers, as well as the performance of your content.

Regularly monitoring this data can help you understand what is and isn't working and make adjustments as needed.

By following these tips, you can gain a better understanding of the performance of your Facebook marketing efforts and make informed decisions to improve their effectiveness.

Chapter – 6 Advanced Tips & Tactics

Let's Begin

A – Using Facebook Live for Real-time Engagement

Using

Facebook Live for

Real-time Engagement

A - Using Facebook Live for Real-time Engagement

Use Facebook Messenger bots:

Messenger bots are automated programs that can communicate with users in real-time and provide information or assistance.

You can use Messenger bots to send personalized messages to users, answer frequently asked questions, and even process orders.

Use Facebook Live:

Facebook Live is a feature that allows you to stream live video on Facebook.

You can use Facebook Live to host events, conduct Q&As, and offer behind-the-scenes looks at your business.

Run a contest or giveaway:

Contests and giveaways can be a great way to generate buzz and engagement on your Facebook page.

Just be sure to follow Facebook's rules and guidelines for running contests (https://www.facebook.com/policies/pages_groups_events/).

Collaborate with influencers:

Partnering with influencers can be a powerful way to reach a larger audience and increase the visibility of your business.

You can work with influencers to create sponsored content or host a giveaway on their page.

By using these advanced tactics, you can take your Facebook marketing efforts to the next level and effectively reach and engage more users.

B – Leveraging Facebook Messenger for Customer Service & Lead Generation

Leveraging Facebook Messenger for Customer Service & Lead Generation

Use Facebook Pixel:

Facebook Pixel is a piece of code that you can add to your website to track the actions of users who visit your site from Facebook.

You can use Facebook Pixel to track conversions, retarget users with ads, and create custom audiences for future campaigns.

Use Facebook Audience Network:

Facebook Audience Network is a network of apps and websites that allow you to show ads to users outside of Facebook.

You can use Audience Network to expand the reach of your ad campaigns and target specific types of users.

Use Facebook dynamic ads:

Dynamic ads are ads that are automatically personalized for each user based on their interests and behaviors.

You can use dynamic ads to show relevant products or services to users and increase the chances of conversion.

Use Facebook Workplace:

Facebook Workplace is a communication and collaboration platform for businesses.

You can use Workplace to connect with your team, share updates and documents, and hold virtual meetings.

By using these advanced tactics, you can further optimize your Facebook marketing efforts and increase the chances of success.

C - Utilizing Facebook's tools for E-Commerce & Lead Generation

Utilizing Facebook's tools for E-Commerce & Lead Generation

C - Utilizing Facebook's tools for E-Commerce & Lead Generation

Use Facebook Marketplace:

Facebook Marketplace is a platform that allows users to buy and sell items

within their local community.

You can use Marketplace to promote your products or services and reach a wider audience.

Use Instagram Shopping:

Instagram Shopping is a feature that allows businesses to tag products in their posts and stories and link them to their website.

You can use Instagram Shopping to drive sales and increase the visibility of your products on Instagram.

Use Facebook App Install ads:

App Install ads are ads that promote a mobile app and allow users to download the app directly from the ad. You can use App Install ads to promote your app and drive downloads.

Use Facebook lead ads:

Lead ads are ads that allow users to sign up for more information or make a purchase without leaving the Facebook app.

You can use lead ads to collect leads or make sales directly on Facebook.

By using these advanced tactics, you can further optimize your Facebook marketing efforts and increase the chances of success.

Chapter – 7 Conclusion

Let's Begin

A - Recap of Key Takeaways for Growing a Startup Business with Facebook Marketing

Facebook Marketing can be a Powerful Tool for Growing your Startup Business.

By creating a business page, developing a content strategy, advertising on the platform, and measuring and analyzing your efforts, you can effectively reach and engage your target audience and achieve your business goals.

There are also a number of AdvancedTtactics, such as

Using :

Messenger bots,

Running Contests and

Collaborating with Influencers

that can help you take your Facebook Marketing Efforts to the Next Level.

By staying up-to-date with the latest features and best practices, you can continue to optimize your Facebook marketing efforts and effectively grow your business on the platform.

B – Next Steps for Continuing to Improve & Evolve your Facebook Marketing Efforts.

Facebook marketing can be an effective way to reach and engage potential customers, generate leads, and drive sales for your startup business.

By creating a well-defined strategy and using the right tools and tactics, you can effectively use Facebook to grow your business and achieve your marketing goals.

It's important to regularly track and analyze the performance of your Facebook marketing efforts and make adjustments as needed to ensure that you are getting the best possible return on your investment.

By staying up-to-date with the latest features and best practices, you can continue to optimize your Facebook marketing efforts and effectively grow your business on the platform.

So, these are the ways in which you can use Facebook Marketing to grow your startup business.

Chapter – 8 Let's Get Connected

Facebook Group Link

https://www.facebook.com/groups/
mastertheartoffbmarketing.chiragmarlecha/

WhatsApp Group Link

https://chat.whatsapp.com/CDR5w2cHzwuFZFFArKrSrc

www.ingramcontent.com/pod-product-compliance
Lightning Source LLC
Chambersburg PA
CBHW042101150726
48005CB00033B/1474